WHO AM I?

DUANE SHERIFF

WHO AM I?

DUANE SHERIFF

COPYRIGHT

CONTENTS

INTRODUCTION 1

WHY IS IDENTITY SO IMPORTANT? 8

FAMILY IDENTIFICATIONS 12

NEW CREATION IDENTITY 21

JESUS AND HIS IDENTITY 25

JESUS AND HIS ID JOURNEY 27

ATTACKS ON IDENTITY 30

JOHN THE BAPTIST 35

WHO ARE YOU? 40

INTRODUCTION

Many people live their whole lives suffering under an identity crisis. They labor under a fallen identity in Adam, an imposed identity from parents or friends, or an identity conformed to the world's image. Only in Christ will people discover who they are and God's plan for their lives. Only in Christ will people overcome the identity confusion that is plaguing our culture.

The church needs to be free from any form of imposed identity. Unlike many of today's corporations/institutions, we cannot fall prey to the cultural pressures and trending ideologies of our time. Institutions that were once established in biblical family values and principles are being uprooted and destroyed because they have sold out to the culture. They are suffering from "Identity Amnesia," forgetting who they are and where they came from, and losing billions of dollars in the process. The church at large has fallen prey to these same cultural pressures, and it has cost us a generation. We need to be rooted and grounded in

Jesus and resist the world trying to conform us into an image that does not glorify God.

Jesus said that we are the salt of the earth and the light of the world. He also declares us to be a city set on a hill (Matt. 5:13-14). He goes on to say in Matthew 5:15-16 KJV, *"Neither do men light a candle, and put it under a bushel, but on a candlestick; and it giveth light unto all that are in the house. Let your light so shine before men that they may see your good works, and glorify your Father which is in heaven."* As effective as the censorship move has been it doesn't compare to the self-censorship of the church. We have put our light under a bushel for fear of rejection, being misjudged, or offending. We must be renewed in our new identity in Christ and not be ashamed of the gospel for it is God's power to save (Rom. 1:16-17).

Paul wrote to a young Pastor Timothy sharing on how we are to conduct ourselves in the house of God; *"...which is the church of the living God the pillar and ground of the truth."* (I Timothy 3:15). Our new identity as the church is one of truth. We are ground zero for the truth; that's who we are. As the body of Christ in and on the earth we are pursuers and preservers of the truth and that truth must be spoken in love for people to grow in Christ (Eph. 4:15). Light and truth are used interchangeably in scripture and connects us to our new identity in Christ as we see here in John 3:21, *"But he who does the truth comes to the light, that his deeds may be clearly seen, that they have been done in God."* Jesus said John was a witness of Him and that witness was true (John 5:33). He then went on to call John a burning and shining lamp (John 5:35).

We cannot reach the world by being conformed to it. We are now children of light in Christ and must shine bright in these darkest of days. Paul sums this truth up in Ephesians 5:8, "For you were once darkness, but now you are light in the Lord (new identity). Walk as children of light." (emphasis added). We are all learning who we are in the Lord and how to walk after the new creation in Christ.

What is Identity? Identity is defined in Merriam Webster as:

- The distinguishing character or personality of a person. Your individuality or personhood.

- The relation established by psychological identification.
- The condition of being the same with something described or asserted.

Who or what we identify with affects our identity. I Corinthians 15:33 says, *"Be not deceived, evil communications corrupt good manners."* Many people are deceived in this regard. They believe they can identify with and hang out with certain groups or people and it have no effect on them or their identity. Proverbs 13:20 declares, *"He who walks with wise men will be wise, but the companion of fools will be destroyed."* Your friends are your future. Peer pressure to conform does not end after high school or college. As parents, we often say to our children, "If your friends jumped off a bridge, would you?" The answer is YES if they are not secure in who they are.

We face similar dilemmas to conform to the ideals of a corrupt culture now, leading us to questions like, "will you celebrate pride month because your co-workers do?" "Will you hang the rainbow flag outside your place of business?" "Will you affirm your child's identity confusion that has been imposed by a corrupt culture?" (Genesis 1:26-28/5:1-2/Mark 10:5-9)

Many times, we are best known and defined by our enemies, those who hate or reject us. Jesus said if people hated Him, they would also hate His followers (Matthew 10:22, Luke 21:17, John 15:18). Who do you identify with? If the answer is Jesus, expect a measure of persecution (II Timothy 3:12).

Identification or who or what we identify with affects or in some cases reflects who we are.

To "identify" according to the Collins English Dictionary means:

- To treat or consider the same.
- To make identical to or similar.
- To associate closely.

There are certain names I could say, and most readers would automatically associate these people with a defining feature of their identity. These names are linked to larger concepts that have shaped their identities. For example, if I say Martin Luther, many people will think of the Protestant

Reformation or the Lutheran Church. Those associations run so deeply that you cannot separate the two. Now, if I say Dr. Martin Luther King, Jr. what associated ideas come to mind? Primarily the Civil Rights movement. Dr. King is the father of the Civil Rights Movement, and that concept is intertwined with his identity. John and Charles Wesley are obviously connected to the Methodist Church. These name associations hold true for numerous examples: Michael Jordan, basketball; Tiger Woods, golf. In the same way, the Church should be closely identified with Jesus in a way that is inseparable. For too long, believers have suffered from identity confusion and amnesia. We have forgotten we have an identification with Jesus in which our identities are to be formed. We are united to Christ and now function as His body in the earth. We are one spirit with the Lord (I Corinthians 6:17) and the very flesh of His flesh and bone of His bones (Ephesians 5:30). When we forget this association with Christ, we've lost our purpose in the earth and our direction in life, which results in brokenness at our core. Christians need a great awakening to our new identity in Christ. Our identification with Him is profound and life altering.

It is in our union with Christ that we discover our purpose in the earth and fulfill God's word and will for our lives. Everything we do comes out of who we believe we are. We are "the body of Christ" in the earth. Jesus is the "head of the body," His church. You cannot separate us from Jesus any more than you can separate Martin Luther King Jr. from the civil rights movement. When I say "Jesus" there is a union associated with the church that must be understood, experienced, and enjoyed. When I say, "the church," you cannot separate a close association with Jesus any more than you can separate your head from your body. How many truly see their new identity in Christ and are identifying with Him?

"I am crucified with Christ: nevertheless I live; yet not I, but Christ liveth in me: and the life which I now live in the flesh I live by the faith of the Son of God, who loved me, and gave himself for me."

Galatians 2:20, KJV

WHY IS IDENTITY SO IMPORTANT?

First, your identity is important because it connects you to your purpose. In the 1960's everyone was searching for self. They asked questions like, "Who am I?;" "Where am I?;" "Where am I going and can I get there from here?." The Bible calls it being lost but we labeled it "the hippie movement." Answers were not found in smoking dope and singing "Kum by yah." The answer then and still is today found in the Cross and faith in Jesus, singing "Amazing Grace." Who are you? You are a child of God, a citizen of the kingdom of God, a world overcomer, the head and not the tail, above and not beneath, blessed coming in and blessed going out; and the list goes on.

Where are you? Seated in heavenly places in Christ. Ephesians 2:4-6 says, *"But God, who is rich in mercy, because of His great love with which He loved us, even when we were dead in trespasses, made us alive together with Christ (by grace you have been saved), and raised us up together, and made us sit together in the heavenly places in Christ Jesus,"* We are now identified with Christ in His death, burial, resurrection, and seating in heavenly places. Where are we going? To heaven and eventually a new heaven and earth where we will rule and reign with Christ forever and yes, we can get there from here!

You are in this world but not of it and need to operate according to God's kingdom principles. God created you on purpose and for a purpose. If the enemy can confuse you in your identity he can destroy your purpose and destiny. You will be unhappy, unfruitful, and unfulfilled in your life. God created us in our mother's womb for a specific purpose (Psalm 139:13-14/ Is. 43:7 & 21 / 44:2 & 21 & 24 / 49:5 / Jer. 1:5). Your divine design by God matches your purpose. The reason you are the way you are is not an accident; it is by design, on purpose, to fulfill a purpose.

Second, your identity sets the course for your life. Your entire life rotates around your identity. Rhythms and routines become conductors on the course of your destiny. The trajectory of your life revolves around who you are. For example, the routines and habits of a doctor will differ from those of a tennis player, but each one is being directed through life by how they identify themselves.

Third, our identity matters because it affects our personhood and wholeness. Identity confusion creates unnecessary emotional and psychological pain. The damage being inflicted on our innocent children in identity and gender confusion is horrifying and has catastrophic consequences. To blur the lines between male and female, identities created by God in wisdom and simplicity, is a travesty. To induce our children to partake of chemical cocktails and hormone blockers has an effect on their developing brains and their personhood. These medications will not and cannot change their God-assigned gender. They will be bound to them for a lifetime. No amount of medication or elective surgeries can change their biological, scientific gender. It can only damage who they are and their purpose in life. Elective reconstructive surgeries and re-assignment surgeries performed on minors should be criminal. God is the Creator and Author of our genders (Genesis 1: 26-29, Mark 10: 5-9). What we see in our culture today is the apex of identity confusion and causes long term, and in some cases, irreversible damage. While I didn't suffer from gender confusion, my identity crises affected my personhood and wholeness as a human being, nonetheless. To a measure all of us have suffered this crises in one degree or another because of sin and Adam. Our fallen condition in Adam damaged us all and can only be fixed and cured in Christ. Our first birth united us to Adam and his sin in the garden, but our new birth has united us to Christ and gives us a new identity that heals our personhood and makes us whole. God's salvation through Christ at the cross involves spirit, soul, and body. God cares about all three parts of our being and person hood. I Thessalonians 5:23-24 states, *"Now may the God of peace Himself sanctify you completely; and may your whole spirit, soul, and body be preserved blameless at the coming of our Lord Jesus Christ. He who calls you is faithful, who also will do it."* God cares about our spirit, soul, and body, and wills to preserve it. God would never want us to mutilate our bodies. All three parts are involved in our personhood.

FAMILY IDENTIFICATIONS

We all have three families that shape our identities: our immediate family, the family of man, and the family of God. Two are inescapable and one is by choice through faith in Jesus and the power of the cross.

IMMEDIATE FAMILY

We all have an identification with our parents and grandparents. This identification was not by choice. We did not ask to be born or choose which family to born into. Each generation carries a genetic identification with our immediate families. The physical features that make up our bodies are shared with our families on a DNA level. Our hair, bone structure, eye and skin color—all of these come from our genetics. Some of these markers that identify us can be changed, but more have to be overcome. For example, I can't change my skin color, I have to overcome any prejudice of any society against me. I can't change my bone structure and its effect on my stature. I have to overcome it in Christ. Whether you are short or tall, it is what it is.

Gender assignment falls under this category as well. It is not fluid or decided upon by us. We are either born male or female and that assignment was predetermined by God. His workmanship is marvelous and creations are wonderful. We now worship God in spirit and truth (John 4:24). We do not worship creation, of which we are a part, but submit to Creator God in love and servanthood. Creator God's design in spirit, soul, and body is for a divine purpose in my life. I am created on purpose for a purpose. Again, we did not choose which family we were born in and can carry some similar genetic traits.

Someone once said one of my daughters looks like her mom. Of course, my response was, "You haven't seen her in a beard." I was trying to take credit for her beauty and I guess the beard would have diminished such beauty. Nonetheless, our children carry some physical traits whether good or bad from their parents. On the outside, we see these shared traits and they become a source of our identities. Phrases like, "he looks like a Sheriff" or "she walks like her mom," show how physical traits can be shared within a family and be identifying markers.

Though the physical traits within families are often easy to see, there are also psychological identifications within families that are not visible but have a big impact. These identifiers are not always healthy or Biblical. For my family of origin, we had an unhealthy association with poverty. The Sheriffs were just poor and that became a part of our family identity. It was who we were. To break out would be an afront to the family. It would make everyone else look bad. If you wanted to succeed and prosper, you were the odd one out. When I got a tennis scholarship to attend college, not everyone in my family celebrated. I could hear the rumblings of "he thinks he's better than us," or "who does he think he is?" echoing within my family's conversations.

Just like my family wanted to conform me into their impoverished image, Christians will face many worldly pressures that aim to conform us into an image other than Christ. When we no longer identify with an identity imposed by our families, we will certainly face pushback. Jesus warned us that following Him would draw dividing lines within our families:

> *"Do not think that I came to bring peace on the earth. I did not come to bring peace, but a sword. For I have come to set a man against his father, a daughter against her mother, and a daughter-in-law against her mother-in-law, and a man's enemies will be those of his own household."*

Matthew. 10:34-36

Jesus continues to say that our love and loyalty to Him should be above all things, including our families and our own lives. This is a part of taking up our cross, experiencing Christian suffering, as we follow Jesus. When we make Jesus Lord and begin to identify with Him, it separates us from all identifications that violate our new nature in Christ. It's not that we don't love and honor our families, it's that we simply love Jesus more. Our new identity in Christ, like a sword, separates us from all inherited and false identities that used to define us. I don't deny or renounce my identification with my earthly family, but I am not controlled by it or locked into any pattern that is contrary to Christ's calling.

FAMILY OF MAN

We are all affected and shaped by the family of man—the human race, whose father is Adam. If we were able to trace our roots back far enough, we were all born through Adam, the father of first creation. We all came out of one man, Adam. The whole human race was on the inside of Adam in the garden. When he sinned, we sinned in him. Where he went, we went. In Adam, we carry an identification with sin, being born into a sin nature. This identity in Adam carries many negative traits, such as guilt, condemnation, judgement, and ultimately death. Scripture teaches that we were all made sinners by one man's disobedience (Romans 5:17-19). We were sinners, not because of sins we committed, but rather because we inherited Adam's sinful nature through birth. Once we see how we received an identification with sin, through Adam's fallen lineage, we see how God makes a way out of sin—through being born again in Christ. It is through faith in Jesus, the second man, the last Adam, that we receive a new and redeemed identity (I Corinthians 15:45, 47).

According to II Corinthians 5:17, a believer's second birth makes them a new creation. If a person believes that their sins make them a sinner, they might wrongly believe that their good works make them righteous. Humans are all born into sin by one man's disobedience (Adam) and must be born again out of sin by one man's obedience (Jesus). The Apostle Paul illustrates this point:

"Do you not know that the unrighteous will not inherit the kingdom of God? Do not be deceived. Neither fornicators, nor idolaters, nor adulterers, nor homosexuals, nor sodomites, nor thieves, nor covetous, nor drunkards, nor revilers, nor extortioners will inherit the kingdom of God. And **such were some of you.** *But you were washed, but you were sanctified, but you were justified in the name of the Lord Jesus and by the Spirit of our God."*

I Corinthians 6:9-11

In Adam, our sin nature looked like this list. These things were not just what we did—it was who we were. In Christ we are now washed, sanctified, and justified so from our new nature and identity in Christ, our actions change as our minds are renewed to God's word (Rom. 12:2). We are no longer condemned in Adam, but now justified in Christ. We are now identified in the family of God, not "The Addams Family." Remember those guys? They thought everyone but their family was strange, and that they were the normal ones. Those in Adam, the family of man, think this way. They believe the sin nature is normal, but the reality is that those in Christ are the normal ones. We did not choose this family either, we only get to choose whether or not to remain in this family. All are born into it, but can now be born again out of it.

FAMILY OF GOD

For the born-again believer, we inherit a whole new identity from a new family. Faith in Christ brings about new family dynamics and traits that didn't exist in our fallen nature. In the family of God, righteousness is our new nature. People living in God's family, seeking the Kingdom of God first, are living according to God's plan for mankind. Adam is the father of first creation where sin and death rule. Jesus is the father of the new creation where life and righteousness rule. Jesus ushers in the opportunity for a new family to define us:

For unto us a Child is born, unto us a Son is given and the government will be upon His shoulder. And His name will be called Wonderful, Counselor, Mighty God, **Everlasting Father***, Prince of Peace.*

Isaiah 9:6

Jesus is not the Heavenly Father, though they are eternally one, but He is the Everlasting Father of the new creation. In Jesus, we are born again of an incorruptible seed (I Peter 1:23). Jesus is the second man, the last Adam, the Everlasting Father of the grace race, the new creation. We are no longer sinners in Adam, but now are saints in Christ. Jesus is called the second man, the last Adam (I Cor. 15:45 / 47). Jesus stood on behalf of us all. We were in Adam in the garden and where He went, we went. We were also with Christ at the cross and where He went, we went.

- He died (we died—Galatians 2:20)
- He was buried (we were buried—Romans 6:4 / Col. 2:12)
- He was raised (we were raised—Ephesians 2:1 & 4-6)

- He was seated (we were seated—Ephesians 2:6)

We were identified with Christ forever changing our identity. He is the last Adam because we will never, ever need another one. Unlike the first man (Adam) who failed and brought sin and death; the second man brought righteousness and life. He is the Everlasting Father of the new creation; it will never end.

NEW CREATION IDENTITY

Therefore, if anyone is in Christ, he is a new creation; old things have passed away; behold, all things have become new.

II Corinthians 5:17

This is a reality in your spirit man. We are a three part being; spirit, soul, and body (I Thess. 5:23). In your new, born-again spirit you are a new creation. The New Living Translation of II Corinthians 5:17 says, *"This means that anyone who belongs to Christ has become a new person... The old life is gone; a new life has begun."* The old person in Adam, a sinner by nature is gone! You are a new person in your spirit man.

We are now in a new family, a new Kingdom, with a new nature, headed for a new heaven and new earth. As new believers in Jesus, we must deal with our old identity in Adam (the flesh) and be renewed in our new identity in Christ (the spirit). We must learn to put off the old man in Adam and to put on the new man in Christ. Paul gives this instruction:

*...that you **put off**, concerning your former conduct, the old man which grows corrupt according to the deceitful lusts, and be renewed in the spirit of your mind, and that you put on the new man which was created according to God, in true righteousness and holiness.*

Ephesians 4:22-24

We have to put off the old man described here as our former conduct / old way of life. Now we put on the new man which is declared righteous and truly holy. How do we do this? Through the renewing of our mind. As we are renewed in the spirit of our minds to our new identity in Christ, our old actions and conduct are put off.

Notice we must be renewed in the spirit of our minds. The spirit of our mind refers to our mental disposition or attitude, how we think and perceive things. How we view ourselves in Christ is different than when we were in Adam. Mind renewal is an arduous process, but necessary for Christian transformation (Romans 12:2). For example, you are no longer a sinner saved by grace. You are now the righteousness of God in Christ because you have been saved by grace. You are no longer dead

in sins and trespasses in Adam (Ephesians 2:5) but dead **to** sin in Christ Jesus (Romans 6:2). You are no longer a victim in life but a victor in Christ (2 Corinthians 2:14 / Romans 8:37 / 1 John 5:4-5). You are no longer children of darkness but now children of the light (Ephesians 5:8). II Corinthians 5:16- 17 addresses this process:

> *Therefore, from now on, we regard no one according to the flesh. Even though we have known Christ according to the flesh, yet now we know Him thus no longer. Therefore, if anyone is in Christ, he is a new creation; old things have passed away; behold, all things have become new.*

> II Corinthians 5:16-17

We should no longer see ourselves after the flesh, but through the lens of new creation, through the spirit. The old things (identity in Adam) have passed away and the new things (identity in Christ) has come. We must renew our minds to these new creation realities in Christ to be transformed. These realities are in our spirit, not our flesh. It is the inner man being renewed, not the outer man (2 Corinthians 4:16).

I used to believe that the disciples had an advantage in following Jesus because they knew Him after the flesh. But even though the disciples walked with Jesus face-to-face, they didn't fully grasp the work He was doing and found themselves doubting His identity at different points. We know that near Jesus' death, one disciple betrayed Him, one denied Him, and the others forsook Him. Before the resurrection and the new creation they only knew Jesus after the flesh. It was after the resurrection and the new birth that their lives were so radically changed. So how do we know Jesus is vital, and it is the key to unlocking how we know ourselves in Christ? And because we do not know Jesus after the flesh, how do we know Him? We know Him through the Scriptures and by the Holy Spirit. This is how we come to know Jesus and come to know our new identities in Christ, after the scriptures and the Holy Spirit.

JESUS AND HIS IDENTITY

How did Jesus know He was the Son of God? Was He merely pretending to be human or did He really enter creation as Creator God made human flesh? Did He fully embrace the human condition independent of sin and really become a baby lying in a manger? When and how did Jesus become aware of His identity? According to the Scriptures, Jesus was 12 years old when he dialogued with the religious leaders of His day, confounding their understanding. Mary and Jospeh had left Him in Jerusalem following the Passover and were more than a day's journey away when they discovered Jesus wasn't with them. They traveled in family clans and with so much extended family they simply missed Him not being among them. His family and extended family came to Jerusalem for the Passover and had left together. When they returned to find Jesus in the temple, Mary said to Him, *"Son why have you done this to us? Look, your father and I have sought you anxiously."* His response gives insight into his self-awareness: *"did you not know I was about **my Father's** business?"* (Luke 2:48-49). By the age of 12, He had discovered that Joseph was not His father but that God was His Father. By this time, the Holy Spirit had spoken to Jesus and revealed who His Father was. His brothers and sisters had no clue. It was the Holy Spirit and the Scriptures who showed Jesus His identity. Mary did not reveal this truth to Him nor did Joseph. Flesh and blood did not reveal His identity any more than flesh and blood could reveal your new identity. When Jesus later asks the disciples who did people say He was the answers varied, maybe Elijah, John the Baptist, Jeremiah, or one of the prophets. But then Jesus asks more directly, *"who do you say that I am?"* Jesus honors Peter's response *"thou art the Christ, the Son of the Living God,"* by saying that flesh and blood did not reveal this truth, but His Father in heaven did (Matthew. 16: 13-17). Neither did flesh and blood reveal to Jesus who He was, and it cannot reveal to us who we are in Christ. Mary nor Joseph ever told Jesus who He was. Our parents cannot reveal to us who we are either. God revealed to Peter who Jesus was and He reveals to us who Jesus is and then who we are in Him.

JESUS AND HIS ID JOURNEY

Jesus spent many hours of His youth in the temple and studying the Scriptures. It was there that the Holy Spirit revealed to Him who His Father was, and thereby who He was. He would be reading the Scriptures and hear the voice of Holy Spirit say, *"that is you!"* Jesus would read about the sacrificial lamb. *"That's you."* He would read about the temple. *"That's you."* You can see through Jesus' own teachings that he found Himself in the Scriptures. In John 5:39 He says, *"You search the Scriptures, for in them you think you have eternal life; and* **these are they** *which testify of Me."* (emphasis added) After His resurrection Jesus met two of His disciples on the road to Emmaus and began a conversation with them. They were reasoning among themselves over the recent events in Jerusalem and the death of Jesus. They didn't recognize that it was Jesus conversing with them and were sad and confused over Jesus' death. Jesus said to them, *"O foolish ones, and slow of heart to believe in all that the prophets have spoken! Ought not the Christ to have suffered these things and to enter into His glory? And beginning at Moses and all the* *prophets, He expounded to them in* **all the scriptures** *the things concerning* **Himself.**" (Luke 24:25-27).

Jesus discovered who He was in scripture beginning at Moses and the writings of the prophets. Isaiah spoke of His death on the cross and God's will to save us from our sins. "*...His life made an offering for sin...*" (Isaiah 53:10 NLT). He gave details of Christ's burial in a rich man's grave (Isaiah 53:9). God spoke to Jesus out of the scriptures who would betray Him and how. Psalm 41:9 says, "*Even my own familiar friend in whom I trusted, Who ate my bread. Has lifted up his heel against me.*" In Psalm 55:12-14 is where Jesus read again it would be a friend betraying Him not an enemy. "*For it is not an enemy who reproaches me; then I could bear it. Nor is it one who hates me who has exalted himself against me; Then I could hide from him. But it was you, a man my equal, My companion and my acquaintance. We took sweet counsel together, And walked in the house of God in the throng.*" The Holy Spirit spoke to Jesus and revealed it would be one of His own disciples to betray Him (Judas).

The writer of Hebrews speaks of Jesus in this way, "*Behold I have come—In the volume of the book it is*

written of Me—*To do Your will, O God."* (Hebrews 10:7).

Jesus saw Himself in the Scriptures by revelation of the Holy Spirit. Likewise, you and I must see ourselves in the Scriptures, after the spirit, as a new creation. God's Word is a mirror of the spirit world and our born-again spirit. *"It is the Spirit who gives life; the flesh profits nothing. The words that I speak to you are spirit, and they are life."* (Jn. 6:63). The volume of the book is the scriptures. God's word reveals the spirit world and who we are in that world or realm. You look in a mirror to discover your flesh (outer man). The word is a mirror revealing your new, born-again spirit (your inner man).

ATTACKS ON IDENTITY

Jesus was attacked in his identity at the beginning and the end of His ministry. The only way to keep Him, or us, from fulfilling our purpose is with an assault on our identities. In Matthew 4, we see Satan tempt Jesus in the wilderness. The first temptation came against Jesus after 40 days of fasting. Satan challenged Him, *"If You are the Son of God, command that these stones become bread."* (Matthew 4:3, emphasis added) The enemy directly confronted His identity using that word "if." If you really are who you say you are, then prove it. Demonstrate it beyond reproof. Satan knew that if He could get Jesus to doubt His identity, he would derail His destiny. Satan then brings Jesus up to the holy city and set Him on the pinnacle of the temple. He challenged again *"If you are the Son of God, throw Yourself down. For it is written: 'He shall give His angels charge over you,' and 'in their hands they shall bear you up, lest you dash your foot against a stone.'"* (Matthew 4:6 emphasis added) Jesus responded by saying, *"It is written again, You shall not tempt the Lord your God"* (Deuteronomy 6:16). Notice again how the attack was against Jesus' identity—if you are God's son, then prove this identity. Satan attacks our identity to try and get us to doubt our purpose and destiny. The final temptation was an invitation to worship Satan versus God:

Again, the devil took Him up on an exceedingly high mountain, and showed Him all the kingdoms of the world and their glory. And he said to Him, "All these things I will give You if You will fall down and worship me." Then Jesus said to him, "Away with you, Satan! For it is written, "You shall worship the Lord your God, and Him only you shall serve."

Matthew 4:8-10

When faced with temptation, Jesus rooted His identity in being a worshipper of the one true God. Even in this third temptation Satan was attacking Jesus' identity. While this was a veiled attack, it was an attack no less. Only in worship of the Creator God, can creation discover its purpose. We are a part of creation that worships Creator God discovering who we are, where we came from, where we are going and how to get there from here. Discovering who we are is found in worship of our Creator God. All of creation finds its purpose in the

Creator. What we worship, we become like. To be like God, we must know what God is like, and that comes out of beholding God in worship. Satan wants to rival God on the throne of our hearts so that he can pervert and confuse our identities. Any false worship leads to identity confusion, because we were designed to be image bearers of God, not any graven image.

The wilderness temptation happened before Jesus began His earthly ministry, but even later, Satan's tactics against Jesus had not changed. This gives us insight into how to counter the assaults of the enemy because his schemes are consistent. Creativity is not one of his hallmarks. In Matthew 27:40, while suffering on the cross, Jesus hears a familiar taunt, *"if you are the Son of God, come down from the cross."* Jesus had the power to come down from the cross, but that would have violated his identity and purpose in life. He was on the cross *because* He was the Son of God, and He came to do the will of His Father; die on the cross for our sins.

In the wilderness Satan tried to get Jesus to prove who He was and Jesus refused. Now Jesus on the cross is proof of who He is and Satan tempts

Him to violate and retreat from His purpose which was connected to His identity. He was the lamb of God (identity) that would take away the sins of the world (purpose and destiny). That could only be done by remaining and hanging on the cross.

As God's Son, He was qualified to die for the sins of the whole world. Only the Son of God, a co-Creator with God according to John 1:3, could ransom His life for all of creation. Later, other voices mock Jesus, saying, *"if He is the King of Israel, let Him now come down from the cross, and we will believe Him"* (Matthew. 27:42 emphasis added). These lies and challenges to Jesus' identity were breathed from the father of lies, Satan (John 8:44). Jesus coming off the cross would not have created faith. It was Jesus dying on the cross and faith in His death, burial, and resurrection that brings us salvation. Remember He is the lamb of God who takes away the sins of the world. His identity (lamb of God) determines His purpose (die for our sins). Once again, Satan was attacking identity in an attempt to destroy destiny.

From the start of Jesus' earthly ministry up unto His death, Satan tried to challenge Jesus' identity. As followers of Jesus, the enemy will do no less to you and me. "If you really are a Christian…" or "If you are a child of God…" may sound like familiar attacks. When we hear these taunts from the enemy, we must overcome like Jesus did, by relying on the Word of God. We must exalt God's Word as final and absolute authority, letting *"God be true but every man a liar"* (Romans 3:4).

JOHN THE BAPTIST

John the Baptist exemplifies what it's like to identify according to God's Word. Luke 1 tells the story of his miraculous birth. He was born to a Zechariah, a priest, and Elizabeth, a barren woman who God favored with a child even in her later years. In their culture and societal structure, they were a privileged people. John could have lived a reasonably comfortable life with his lineage, but instead, he chose to dwell in the wilderness. It was in the wilderness that the Holy Spirit called John and he began to preach a baptism of repentance for the remission of sin (Luke 3:3). According to Matthew 3:4, John wore clothes of camel's hair with a leather belt, and he ate locusts and wild honey. This description paints him as a unique character, and his message was a simple one—repent, for the Kingdom is at hand (Matthew. 3:2). While he called sinners to repentance, he called out the Pharisees. This did not set well with the religious leaders of His day.

The gospel of John records an instance where a delegation of priests and Levites from Jerusalem question John about his identity and his authority:

"Who are you?" He confessed, and did not deny, but confessed, "I am not the Christ." And they asked him, "What then? are you Elijah?" He said, "I am not." "Are you the Prophet?" And he answered, "No." Then they said to him, "Who are you, that we may give an answer to those who sent us? What do you say about yourself?"

John 1:19-22

How do you identify? This is what the religious leaders of Jerusalem wanted to know. Four times He was asked; "Who are you?" Then they asked, "What do you say about yourself?" In other words, how do you identify?

John could have given a multitude of responses or answers. He could have said he was the son of the priest, Zechariah, or the miracle child of Elizabeth who was barren. He could have identified as the Messiah's cousin because of Elizabeth's relation to Mary. He could have identified Himself after the flesh and by many natural markers But how did John answer the question, "who are you?" According to John 1:23, John answers *"I am 'the voice of one crying out in the wilderness: "Make straight the way of the LORD,"'* as the prophet Isaiah said." When asked about his identity, John quotes Isaiah 40:3. John had been studying the Scriptures and heard the Holy Spirit speaking, *"that is you."* He discovered who he was in the Scriptures, by the Holy Spirit, as you and I will in the New Testament. John went on to point people to the Messiah even as we do because of our identity in Christ.

This is how my personal journey began in May 1980. I was in a backslidden condition when I met my wife Sue for the first time. God had spoken to her that she would witness to me and our paths finally crossed. The story is too long to share the whole experience but here is the bottom line. After eight to nine hours of sharing God's love and forgiveness for me, I repented of my sin and then had an open vision of the cross. I saw Jesus on the cross, but I saw me inside of Him. I saw my identification with Him on the cross. I saw God punish Jesus for all my sins and when He died, I died. When He was buried, I was buried and when He was raised, I was raised. The amazing thing is that the me in Him after the resurrection was a different me than the one who died with Him on the Cross, and was buried with Him. I then saw Him ascend to Heaven and seated in heavenly places and I too was in Him. He then told me that we would rule and reign together forever. This experience shook me to the core and I had to know if it was true and in the Bible. Anyone can have a vision but I needed to know this was real and God speaking to me. I spent the next three months searching the scriptures to bring meaning and understanding to what I had seen. To my amazement and delight, I discovered that it was the gospel! (Jesus' death, burial, resurrection, and our identity with Him). Sure enough, Paul said in Galatians 2:20 (KJV)— *"I am **crucified with Christ**: nevertheless I live; yet not I (the old me in Adam), but Christ liveth in me…"* (the new me in Christ). Then I read in Romans 6:3-4— *"…we were baptized into his death. Therefore we are **buried with him** by baptism into death…"* Then in Ephesians 2:6— *"and hath **raised us up together**, and made us **sit together** in heavenly places in Christ Jesus."* To complete the revelation I discovered in Romans 5:17— *"…much more they which receive abundance of grace and of the gift of righteousness shall reign in life by one, Jesus*

Christ." As I am reading these passages, the Holy Spirit is speaking to me, "That's you Duane." Since that time, I have not questioned my identity or struggled with God's love and forgiveness for me.

WHO ARE YOU?

How do you identify? If we haven't heard this question, we haven't been keeping up with the enemy's tactics in our world gone awry. What are our preferred pronouns? How should Christians answer this question? Many born-again believers do not know how to answer this question and can be as confused as the world. I no longer identify with my old man in Adam who had a sin nature. I no longer live in Adam, dead in sins and trespasses (Ephesians 2:1). I'm not a sinner saved by grace. I was a sinner in Adam, and I am saved by grace, but I'm righteous now in Christ (a saint) still saved by grace. My "authentic self" in Adam is dead and my new self is in Christ. I'm a new creation in Christ (II Corinthians 5:17) and I no longer identify with Adam or the world; I've been crucified to both (Galatians 6:14-15). My preferred pronouns are more than a conqueror through Him who loved me and gave Himself for me (Romans 8:37). I'm a world overcomer (I John 5:4). I'm a victor, not a victim (II Corinthians 2:14). I'm the head and not the tail (Deuteronomy 28:13). I'm blessed with all spiritual blessings in the heavenly places (Ephesians 1:3). You may call me a Chrisitan because Christ in me is the hope of glory (Colossians 1:27). My new identity is in Christ and Him crucified (Galatians 2:20 and Philippians 1:21).

Because of Christ's sacrifice and the Holy Spirit's work to reveal my true nature, I no longer labor under a fallen identity in Adam. In Christ, I'm free from guilt, shame, insecurities, inferiorities, and complexes. Condemnation is no longer a part of my personhood (Romans 8:1). I've repented of my "authentic self" dead in sins and trespasses in Adam and only celebrate my new self in Christ. We are being transformed by the renewing of our minds to this new creation (Romans 12:2). Renew your mind to all the new creation realities and then set it on things above (Colossians 3:1). The new you, the real "authentic you," is righteous and truly holy. Who are you? The forgiven, the washed in the blood, the redeemed of the Lord, the apple of God's eye. You are one spirit with the Lord (I Corinthians 6:17). You are forever a member of His beloved family and so much more.

SALVATION PRAYER

If your heart desires connection with your Heavenly Father and to live in the blessing of His family, there is hope in Christ Jesus. If you have not made Jesus Lord of your life but would like to do so, you can simply pray this:

"Father, I come to you today; I confess I'm not right, but I want to be right and make things right. I cannot do enough or quit enough to save myself, I need help. I believe Jesus is that help. I believe He came to this earth, lived a perfect life, and died on the cross for me. He bore my sins and the punishment for all my sins. He died, was buried, and rose again on the third day. I now confess Him as Lord, King, and Savior. Thank you for forgiving me and cleansing me of all my sin and changing me in my heart. Help me now to serve you all the days of my life, with all my heart. Amen!"

If you prayed this prayer and received Jesus in your heart today, let us know and we will send you a free book! Contact us at 580-634-5665 or dsm@pastorduane.com

Scan to Watch

GRACE
&TRUTH

oin Duane as he boldly teaches Biblical
visdom mixed with his unique sense of
umor, offering hope & revelation for
oday's world.

ABOUT THE AUTHOR

Duane Sheriff is in author, international speaker and the Founding Pastor / Senior Elder of Victory Life Church, a multi-campus church which is headquartered in Durant, OK. Duane travels the world speaking at conferences, and churches, and is a frequent teacher at Charis Bible College. He has a passion to help people discover their identity in Christ and help them be transformed through the Word of God. His first book, *Identity Theft*, was released in 2017. Since then he has authored several more books including: *Our Union with Christ, Better Together,* and *Counterculture*. Duane and his wife, Sue, have been married since 1980 and together have four children and are blessed with many grandchildren. For additional free teachings visit our website at **www.pastorduane.com**

CONTACT INFORMATION

Duane Sheriff Ministries

PO Box 427, Durant, OK

dsm@pastorduane.com

Helpline (Mon. – Fri. 8am-5pm CT)

580-404-0376

www.pastorduane.com

Made in the USA
Middletown, DE
20 May 2025